Borrowed Futures

The Hidden Cost of College
Debt—and How to Turn It
into a Strategic Advantage

Author/Editor: Rev. Darryl Bass

Electronic ISBN: 978-1-972115-12-1 (EPUB)
                 978-1-972115-32-9 (Kindle)
Paperback ISBN: 978-1-972115-13-8
Printed in the United States

The Library of Congress Control Number: 2026906709

Bass Publishing, LLC
Maywood, IL 60153

Disclaimer

The information contained in this book is for educational and informational purposes only. It is not intended as financial, legal, tax, medical, psychological, or professional advice. The author and publisher make no guarantees regarding the results that may be obtained from the use of this material.

All examples provided are illustrative and are not intended to represent or guarantee that any individual will achieve similar results. Personal growth, financial improvement, and life progression outcomes depend on individual effort, discipline, decisions, and circumstances.

Readers are encouraged to seek qualified professional advice regarding financial planning, legal matters, mental health, or other specialized areas before making decisions based on the information provided in this book.

The author and publisher disclaim any liability for any loss, risk, or damages, direct or indirect, that may arise from the use or application of the information contained herein.

By reading this book, you acknowledge that you are responsible for your own decisions, actions, and results.

Details in any stories and anecdotes have been changed to protect the identities of the person(s) involved.

Acknowledgement

First and always, I acknowledge **God**—the source of wisdom, provision, and purpose. Nothing written in these pages exists apart from His grace, His guidance, and His patience with my own growth. Every lesson learned, every system developed, and every truth shared is rooted in His faithfulness and instruction.

I am grateful for the students, families, and individuals whose real-life struggles with debt and financial confusion inspired this work. Your questions, setbacks, and victories gave this book its voice.

I also acknowledge the educators, mentors, and leaders who labor daily to prepare students for success, often without the tools or resources they themselves wish they had. Your work matters more than you know.

Finally, I acknowledge the future readers of this book. Your willingness to learn early, question systems, and take responsibility for your financial life is proof that change is not only possible—it is already happening.

Dedication

This book is dedicated to **my two college legacy students,**
my daughter **Cayleen Bass** and my
granddaughter **DayShawna Brown**.

You are the reason this message matters.

Every word written here carries my desire for you
to walk through college with clarity instead of
confusion, confidence instead of fear, and
freedom instead of financial bondage. This book
is my way of ensuring that education empowers
you without imprisoning your future.

All proceeds from this book are dedicated to
supporting your college education—not just
financially, but intentionally. May this work stand
as a reminder that your legacy is protected, your
future is planned for, and your journey matters
beyond a degree.

May you graduate not only educated, but equipped.
Not only accomplished, but free.

Foreword

College is one of the most formative seasons of life, yet it is also one of the most financially misunderstood. Students are taught how to enroll, how to borrow, and how to succeed academically—but rarely how to protect their future from the silent weight of unmanaged debt.

This book exists to correct that imbalance.

The purpose of these pages is not to shame students for borrowing or to discourage education. It is to provide what is often missing: **truth, strategy, and perspective**. Debt is not inherently evil—but ignorance is expensive. When students understand money early, they gain options that many adults spend decades trying to recover.

The goal of this book is simple but powerful: To help students graduate with awareness, discipline, and direction.

If this book saves one student from unnecessary stress, years of repayment, or financial regret, then it has fulfilled its assignment.

Table of Contents

Acknowledgement v

Dedication vii

Foreword ix

Introduction: You're Not Broke—You're
Uninformed xiii

The Illusion of "Free Money" 1

Lifestyle Inflation on a Student Budget.................9

The Credit Card Trap..17

Student Loans: The Good, the Bad, and the
Dangerous 25

Emotional Debt: The Cost You Don't See 33

Debt as a Tool, Not a Lifestyle.............................39

Strategic Borrowing During College 45

Building Credit Without Destroying Your Future
....51

Leveraging Campus Resources Instead of Debt.57

The Power of Cash Flow While in School 63

Exit Strategy: Graduating Without Panic.............69

Debt Elimination vs. Debt Optimization 75

Designing a Debt-Light, Power-Driven Future..81

Closing Reflection...86

Introduction: You're Not Broke — You're Uninformed

College is often described as an investment—but few students are taught how to calculate the return.

Most students enter college full of ambition, potential, and hope. They leave with knowledge, credentials, and—often—debt they don't fully understand. This debt doesn't just affect finances; it shapes choices, delays milestones, and quietly limits freedom long after graduation day.

This book was written to interrupt that cycle.

You don't need to fear debt—but you do need to understand it. You need to know how it works, how it grows, how it influences behavior, and how it can either serve your future or sabotage it. More importantly, you need to know how to use wisdom when debt is presented—and how to walk away when it isn't necessary.

This is not a book about perfection.
It is a book about preparation.

Inside these chapters, you'll learn how debt quietly enters student life, how lifestyle pressure and emotion amplify it, and how to strategically control, limit, and outgrow it. You'll also learn how to build cash flow, credit, and confidence—so that graduation feels like alignment, not anxiety.

Whether you are a freshman just beginning, a senior preparing to exit, or someone already navigating repayment, this book meets you where you are.

Your financial future is not determined by your starting point.

It is determined by the decisions you make once you know better.

And now—you do.

Chapter 1

The Illusion of "Free Money"

Most college students don't wake up one day and decide to ruin their financial future.
They simply sign paperwork they don't yet understand.

For many students, debt enters their life quietly—without drama, urgency, or fear. It doesn't arrive with flashing warning signs or sleepless nights. It shows up as an email notification, a financial aid award letter, or a signature line that promises opportunity, not obligation. The language sounds harmless. Helpful, even. *Aid. Assistance. Support. Deferred repayment.* None of it feels dangerous in the moment.

And that's exactly the problem.

Student debt is uniquely deceptive because it disconnects action from consequence. Unlike a credit card swipe that immediately reduces your bank balance, student loans create a **delay between decision and discomfort**. You borrow today, but you don't feel the weight until years later—after graduation, after life has already begun asking more of you than you expected.

By the time reality arrives, the debt is no longer optional.

The illusion begins with how the money is presented. Student loans are rarely framed as debt. They're packaged as part of a "financial aid" experience, bundled together with grants and scholarships. When everything shows up on the same award letter, it all feels equally beneficial. But loans are not gifts. They are contracts—

binding agreements that assume your future income will cooperate with your plans.

No one explains what happens if it doesn't.

At eighteen or nineteen, most students are still learning who they are. They are choosing majors, testing independence, and discovering their limits. Asking someone at this stage of life to predict their earning power ten years into the future is unrealistic—yet that is exactly what borrowing requires. Every loan assumes stability, employment, and income growth. Life does not always comply.

What makes student loans especially dangerous is not the borrowing itself, but the **absence of urgency** attached to it. There is no immediate repayment. No monthly bill. No phone call reminding you that interest is accruing quietly in the background. This delay trains the mind to treat the debt as unreal—almost imaginary.

But interest never forgets.

Even while you're sitting in class, studying for exams, or enjoying campus life, your balance may be growing. For unsubsidized loans, interest accrues daily. It compounds silently, patiently, and consistently. The student feels no pain, but the balance keeps score.

This creates what can be called **deferred financial trauma**—a burden postponed, not prevented.

Another layer of the illusion is emotional. Student loans are often justified with hopeful language: *"This is an investment in yourself."* And while education can absolutely be an investment, not every dollar borrowed produces a return. Borrowing without strategy turns education into an expense with interest attached.

The danger is not education—it's **borrowing without intention.**

4

Many students borrow not only for tuition, but for lifestyle. Refund checks become spending money. Loans help cover meals, entertainment, travel, clothing, and conveniences that feel small in the moment but become expensive memories later. Because the money doesn't feel earned, it doesn't feel scarce. And when money doesn't feel scarce, discipline disappears.

The student tells themselves, *"I'll deal with it later."* Later arrives faster than expected.

Grace periods expire. Bills begin. Careers start slower than planned. Entry-level salaries collide with adult responsibilities—rent, transportation, insurance, food. Suddenly, the money that once felt invisible demands attention, and the borrower realizes they are paying for a version of themselves who didn't yet know better.

This is not failure.
This is lack of education.

Debt becomes dangerous when it is entered blindly. But when understood early, it can be approached with wisdom, restraint, and strategy. The goal of this chapter is not to scare you away from borrowing altogether, but to strip away the illusion so you can see clearly.

Debt is not free.
Debt is not neutral.
Debt is always directional—it either moves you forward or holds you back.

Before you borrow another dollar, you must understand what you are agreeing to. You are not just borrowing money—you are borrowing against your future time, income, and flexibility. Every dollar you take today reduces your margin tomorrow unless it is intentionally leveraged to increase your capacity later.

The good news is this: awareness changes outcomes.

Students who understand debt early make better decisions. They borrow less. They borrow smarter. They graduate with options instead of panic. They treat loans as tools—not entitlements—and tools used correctly can build something powerful.

This chapter is your wake-up call, not your condemnation.

If you are already in debt, this book will help you navigate it wisely. If you are about to borrow, it will help you slow down, think critically, and choose intentionally. Either way, you are no longer uninformed—and that alone changes everything.

In the next chapter, we'll explore how college culture quietly pressures students into spending more than they can afford—and how lifestyle decisions, not tuition alone, often become the real source of financial struggle.

You're not behind.
You're becoming aware.
And awareness is the first step toward financial power.

Chapter 2

Lifestyle Inflation on a Student Budget

Debt during college rarely starts with desperation. It starts with normalization.

From the moment students step onto campus, they enter an environment where spending feels justified, expected, and even necessary. Everyone seems to be buying something—food, clothes, technology, experiences. The culture subtly communicates that this is what college life looks like. And when spending becomes part of belonging, restraint begins to feel like deprivation.

This is how lifestyle inflation takes root—not after graduation, but during it.

Lifestyle inflation occurs when your spending increases faster than your income. For students, this imbalance is especially dangerous because income is often limited, inconsistent, or nonexistent, while access to borrowed money creates the illusion of capacity. The presence of funds is mistaken for permission.

Just because money is available does not mean it is affordable.

College introduces independence quickly. Many students are managing money on their own for the first time. Without parental oversight or clear financial education, decisions are driven by emotion, convenience, and comparison. Small choices—daily coffee, food delivery, weekend outings—don't feel significant on their own. But habits compound faster than interest.

What feels like a normal lifestyle in the moment becomes an unsustainable one over time.

Technology intensifies this effect. With payment apps, stored cards, and one-click purchases, spending becomes frictionless. When there is no pause between desire and purchase, discipline rarely enters the conversation. Borrowed money flows as easily as earned money, and the brain does not distinguish between the two.

This is where many students begin funding a lifestyle their future income hasn't yet earned.

Comparison plays a powerful role. College environments bring together students from vastly different financial backgrounds, yet the surface appearance often looks the same. The student with wealthy parents and the student living on loans may dress similarly, eat in the same places, and share the same social spaces. What is invisible is how each person is paying for it.

When financial context is hidden, imitation becomes dangerous.

Many students quietly believe they are falling behind if they are not participating fully. They feel pressure to keep up—to look successful, connected, and comfortable. But no one posts their loan balance. No one advertises their future repayment schedule. The cost is deferred, and the appearance is immediate.

Debt thrives in environments where image matters more than sustainability.

Another overlooked factor is emotional spending. College is stressful. Academic pressure, social adjustment, uncertainty about the future, and identity formation all happen at once. Spending becomes a coping mechanism. A meal out feels like relief. A purchase feels like reward. A trip feels like escape.

These decisions are rarely about money. They are about emotion.

When spending is used to soothe stress or affirm worth, it becomes repetitive and subconscious. Over time, students begin to associate spending with comfort, success, and self-care. The problem is not enjoying life—it's financing joy with tomorrow's income.

Borrowing to maintain emotional balance is one of the most expensive habits a student can form.

Lifestyle inflation is especially dangerous because it rarely feels irresponsible. It feels reasonable. Students tell themselves they'll cut back later, once they graduate or start earning more. But habits formed under pressure don't disappear automatically. They follow you into your first job, your first apartment, and your first real paycheck.

If spending grows with access instead of income, debt becomes permanent.

The truth is this: college is not a rehearsal for adult life—it is the foundation of it. The financial patterns you practice now will shape how you respond to money later. Learning to live below your means while your means are limited builds

14

discipline that creates freedom when your income increases.

Restraint is not punishment.
It is preparation.

Students who resist lifestyle inflation gain an advantage that compounds long after graduation. They experience less stress, more flexibility, and greater confidence. They make decisions based on purpose instead of pressure. And when opportunities arise, they are not weighed down by obligations they can't escape.

This chapter is not calling you to isolation or deprivation. It is calling you to awareness. You don't have to reject every invitation or deny yourself every experience. But you must understand what your lifestyle costs—not just today, but tomorrow.

Your future does not need to finance your present approval.

In the next chapter, we'll examine one of the most common tools used to fund lifestyle inflation on campus—the credit card—and why it quietly reshapes financial behavior faster than any other form of debt.

Awareness changes direction.
Direction determines outcome.

Chapter 3

The Credit Card Trap

Credit cards don't feel dangerous when you first get them.
They feel empowering.

For many college students, a credit card represents adulthood, independence, and trust. It arrives with congratulatory language — *"You're approved."* The limit feels like opportunity. The card feels like freedom. There is no lecture about risk, no explanation of long-term consequences, and no warning that this small piece of plastic can quietly reshape your financial future.

Credit cards are not designed to hurt you.
They are designed to profit from you.

17

Credit card companies aggressively pursue college students because they understand one critical truth: financial habits formed early tend to stick. A student who learns to rely on revolving credit at nineteen is likely to still rely on it at thirty. The industry is not betting on your failure—it is betting on your consistency.

The trap begins with convenience. A credit card removes friction from spending. You don't need cash. You don't need to check your balance. You don't even need to feel the cost. The purchase is separated from the payment, and that separation weakens awareness.

When pain is delayed, restraint disappears.

Minimum payments deepen the illusion. Paying $35 on a $1,200 balance feels manageable. It feels responsible. But minimum payments are not designed to help you get out of debt—they are designed to keep you in it. Most of that payment goes toward interest, not the balance. The debt remains, and the clock keeps ticking.

Interest is the price of patience—and it compounds relentlessly.

What makes credit cards particularly dangerous for students is how quickly balances grow. Emergencies, textbooks, food, travel, and "just this once" purchases pile up faster than expected. Because the limit feels generous and the consequences feel distant, the card becomes a financial crutch.

Soon, the card is no longer used for emergencies—it becomes a lifestyle supplement.

Another hidden danger is how credit cards alter behavior. Studies consistently show that people spend more when using credit than when using cash. The psychological weight of money is lighter when it's borrowed. Each swipe feels small, but the total grows large.

Credit cards don't create overspending. They make it easier to ignore it.

Many students believe they are building credit by carrying a balance. This is one of the most damaging myths in personal finance. You do not need debt to build credit—you need **consistency and discipline**. Carrying balances does not help your score. It helps the lender collect interest.

20

The truth is simple: interest is optional, but ignorance is expensive.

Credit cards also introduce a dangerous cycle of emotional dependence. When money is tight, the card provides relief. When stress increases, the card offers comfort. Over time, the brain associates spending with security. This connection turns a financial tool into an emotional crutch—and emotional debt always outlasts financial debt.

By the time students recognize the pattern, the habit is already formed.

This does not mean credit cards should be avoided entirely. When used intentionally, they can be powerful tools for building credit, tracking expenses, and creating financial leverage. But intention is the dividing line between control and captivity.

A credit card should serve you—not the other way around.

The students who win with credit cards treat them as transactional tools, not supplemental income. They pay balances in full. They understand utilization. They monitor their behavior. Most importantly, they never use credit to solve problems that discipline should address.

Credit is not a solution to under-earning, over-spending, or emotional stress.

The goal is not fear—it is mastery. Understanding how credit works removes its power to control you. When you understand interest, limits, utilization, and repayment, the card becomes neutral. It no longer dictates your choices.

The earlier this mastery begins, the stronger your financial future becomes.

In the next chapter, we'll take a deeper look at student loans—what makes them different from other forms of debt, when they can be beneficial, and when they quietly become one of the most dangerous financial commitments a student can make.

Knowledge creates freedom.
Discipline protects it.

Chapter 4

Student Loans: The Good, the Bad, and the Dangerous

Student loans are often described as *necessary*.
Rarely are they described as *powerful*.

Unlike credit cards, student loans carry an air of legitimacy. They are tied to education, future earning potential, and long-term growth. Because of this, they are often accepted without resistance or scrutiny. Students are told that borrowing is normal, expected, and unavoidable. For many, questioning student loans feels like questioning college itself.

But student loans are not neutral.
They are tools—and tools can build or destroy depending on how they're used.

25

What makes student loans unique is not just their size, but their structure. These loans follow you through life in ways other debt often does not. They are difficult to discharge, long-lasting, and deeply integrated into your financial identity. Once accepted, they become part of your future whether your plans succeed or change.

The first distinction most students are never taught is the difference between **good borrowing and dangerous borrowing**. Not all student loans are harmful. Borrowing to gain skills that reliably increase income can be strategic. Borrowing to support a lifestyle, avoid work, or delay responsibility is not.

The danger lies in borrowing without clarity.

Federal student loans are often framed as safer, and in many ways they are. They offer fixed interest rates, flexible repayment options, and protections during hardship. Subsidized loans delay interest while you're in school. Unsubsidized loans do not. This difference alone can add thousands of dollars to a balance before graduation—yet many students cannot explain which type they have.

When you don't understand the terms, you can't control the outcome.

Private student loans introduce a different level of risk. They are based on credit, often require co-signers, and come with fewer protections. Interest rates can be higher and variable. Repayment terms are less forgiving. While they may fill funding gaps, they often create long-term pressure that limits flexibility after graduation.

What feels like relief today can become restrictions tomorrow.

Another overlooked danger is over-borrowing. Many students accept the full loan amount offered, assuming it reflects what they *need*. In reality, award letters often reflect eligibility, not necessity. The system does not stop you from borrowing more than your future income can comfortably repay.

Approval is not endorsement.

Borrowing also becomes dangerous when it is disconnected from return. Not all degrees yield the same financial outcomes. This does not mean some fields lack value—but it does mean borrowing should be proportional to realistic earning expectations. Taking on high debt for low-income pathways requires a clear plan, not blind hope.

Hope is not a repayment strategy.

Student loans become especially harmful when they remove urgency. Because repayment is delayed, students feel no immediate pressure to minimize balances. Interest accrues quietly. Balances grow invisibly. By the time repayment begins, the debt has already hardened into a long-term obligation.

This is how manageable borrowing becomes overwhelming burden.

Yet student loans are not automatically the enemy. When approached strategically, they can be leveraged. Borrowing to complete a degree faster, gain certifications with strong market demand, or avoid interruptions that delay graduation can reduce total cost over time. The key is intentionality.

Every borrowed dollar should have a job.

Students who succeed with student loans ask different questions before signing:

- Will this loan increase my earning capacity?
- Is there a lower-cost alternative?
- Can I reduce borrowing through work, grants, or scholarships?
- Do I understand how interest will affect the total cost?

These questions create awareness—and awareness creates control.

The goal is not to graduate debt-free at all costs. The goal is to graduate **debt-aware**, debt-prepared, and debt-positioned. When loans are understood and limited, they do not dictate your future—they support it.

In the next chapter, we'll explore a form of debt that rarely appears on a balance sheet but influences spending behavior more than any loan—the emotional patterns that quietly drive financial decisions.

Understanding money starts with understanding yourself.

Chapter 5

Emotional Debt: The Cost You Don't See

Not all debt shows up on a statement.
Some of the most expensive debt is emotional.

Many college students believe their financial challenges are about income, tuition, or bad luck. In reality, money decisions are rarely just mathematical. They are emotional responses to stress, pressure, identity, and unmet needs. Long before a dollar is spent, a feeling has already made the decision.

Emotional debt is created when spending becomes a coping mechanism rather than a choice.

College is a season of transition. Students are navigating independence, academic expectations, social belonging, and uncertainty about the future—all at once. In this environment, money often becomes a tool for emotional regulation. A purchase offers comfort. A night out offers escape. New clothes offer confidence. None of these choices are inherently wrong, but when they are funded by debt, they leave a residue that lingers long after the moment passes.

The relief is temporary.
The obligation is not.

Emotional spending often hides behind reasonable justifications. *"I'm stressed." "I deserve this." "Everyone else is doing it."* These statements feel logical in the moment, but they mask a deeper pattern—using money to soothe what discipline, rest, or support should address.

Debt becomes the bridge between discomfort and relief.

Over time, this pattern conditions behavior. The brain learns to associate spending with comfort and borrowing with safety. When stress appears, the solution feels automatic. This is how financial habits form quietly and solidify quickly.

Emotional debt compounds faster than interest.

Another contributor is identity-based spending. Many students are shaping who they believe they are and who they want to become. Money becomes a way to project confidence, success, or belonging—even when those qualities are still being developed internally. Spending fills the gap between who you are and who you think you should be.

Borrowing to look successful delays becoming secure.

Emotional debt is also reinforced by comparison. Social media highlights experiences, aesthetics, and lifestyles without context. Students measure themselves against curated images and feel pressure to keep up. The spending that follows is rarely about enjoyment—it's about validation.

Validation purchased with debt always expires.

What makes emotional debt especially dangerous is that it feels justified. Unlike reckless spending, it often appears thoughtful, even necessary. But debt taken on to manage feelings creates a cycle where emotions dictate finances instead of finances supporting life goals.

36

This cycle continues until awareness interrupts it.

Breaking emotional debt patterns does not require perfection—it requires honesty. Students must learn to pause and ask why they are spending, not just what they are buying. When emotions are acknowledged instead of numbed, financial decisions become clearer.

Money should support your life, not anesthetize it.

The most financially stable graduates are not those who never felt pressure or stress. They are those who learned to process emotions without financing them. They built resilience before income increased. They developed self-control before access expanded.

This is a skill—and skills can be learned.

Emotional awareness is not a weakness in financial strategy. It is a strength. When you understand your triggers, money loses its power to control you. Debt stops being a reflex and becomes a decision.

In the next chapter, we'll shift from warning to empowerment—exploring how debt, when understood and limited, can be used as a tool rather than a trap.

Freedom begins where awareness replaces impulse.

Chapter 6

Debt as a Tool, Not a Lifestyle

Debt becomes dangerous when it is normalized. It becomes powerful when it is controlled.

Up to this point, we have explored how debt quietly enters a student's life—through convenience, pressure, emotion, and lack of awareness. Now it is time to make an important shift. Debt itself is not the villain. Misuse is. When understood and limited, debt can serve a purpose without becoming a prison.

The difference is intention.

A tool is something you use to build something else. A lifestyle is something you depend on for survival or identity. Many students are never taught this distinction, so borrowing becomes a default response instead of a strategic choice. Debt stops serving a goal and starts funding a way of life.

Tools are temporary.
Lifestyles are permanent.

When debt is treated as a tool, it is connected to a clear outcome. It has a beginning, a purpose, and an end. When debt becomes a lifestyle, it has none of those things. It simply exists, rolling from one season of life into the next, growing heavier with time.

This is why clarity matters more than income.

Strategic debt is used to accelerate progress, not replace discipline. It supports education that increases earning potential. It bridges short gaps that prevent disruption. It solves specific problems with measurable returns. Once the purpose is fulfilled, the debt is eliminated.

Lifestyle debt, on the other hand, sustains comfort, image, and convenience. It fills emotional gaps, extends habits, and delays responsibility. It does not create growth—it creates dependency.

The outcomes are radically different.

Students who learn to use debt strategically begin asking different questions. They consider the total cost, not just the monthly payment. They evaluate how long the debt will last compared to how long the benefit remains. They understand that borrowing today is borrowing time from tomorrow.

Time is the real currency.

Using debt well requires restraint, not access. Just because credit is available does not mean it should be used. Approval is not permission—it is opportunity, and opportunity must be handled wisely.

The most powerful financial skill a student can develop is the ability to say no.

This does not mean avoiding all borrowing. It means borrowing with boundaries. Debt should never be used to maintain a lifestyle you cannot afford with income. It should never be used to escape discomfort or avoid growth. And it should never be used without a clear exit plan.

Every debt should come with a finish line.

When debt is used correctly, it creates leverage. It allows students to invest in themselves without

42

sacrificing long-term stability. It supports progress instead of postponing it. It creates options rather than obligations.

But leverage without discipline becomes collapse.

The goal is not to be debt-free at all costs—it is to be debt-intelligent. Students who master this early graduate with confidence instead of fear. They understand how money works. They are not controlled by access, pressure, or emotion.

They use debt once—and only when it serves them.

In the next chapter, we will explore what strategic borrowing looks like during college—how to decide when borrowing makes sense, when it doesn't, and how to ensure that every dollar borrowed is working toward a measurable future return.

Tools build futures.
Lifestyles drain them.

Chapter 7

Strategic Borrowing During College

Borrowing becomes dangerous when it is automatic.
It becomes strategic when it is deliberate.

Most students borrow because the option exists, not because the outcome is clear. Loans are accepted quickly, often without reflection, because the process feels routine. But strategic borrowing requires slowing down long enough to ask whether the debt will serve your future—or simply follow you into it.

Strategy begins with purpose.

Strategic borrowing is not about avoiding debt entirely. It is about using debt to remove barriers that block progress while refusing to use it for convenience, comfort, or image. The question is never *"Can I borrow?"* The real question is *"What will this borrowing produce?"*

If the debt does not increase your capacity, it is costing you more than money.

One of the most important principles of strategic borrowing is return on investment. Every dollar borrowed should be connected to a realistic outcome—greater earning potential, faster completion, or reduced long-term cost. Borrowing to shorten time to graduation often saves money. Borrowing to delay discipline rarely does.

Time matters more than totals.

Students who borrow strategically understand that staying enrolled and finishing efficiently is often cheaper than stopping and restarting. Extending college by semesters or years increases tuition, living expenses, and opportunity cost. In some cases, limited borrowing prevents larger financial losses later.

But this only works when borrowing is controlled.

Another critical element of strategy is proportionality. Borrowing should align with expected income. This does not mean choosing a career solely for money, but it does require honesty. If future income will be modest, borrowing must be minimal. Large debt paired with limited income creates stress that limits freedom and choices.

47

Debt should expand options—not narrow them.

Strategic borrowers also distinguish between education and experience. While both matter, only one reliably produces financial return. Borrowing to gain marketable skills, certifications, or credentials can be wise. Borrowing to fund experiences, lifestyle upgrades, or social participation rarely is.

Memories fade.
Balances remain.

Work is another often-ignored strategy. Many students avoid employment because borrowing feels easier. But income earned during college reduces debt, builds discipline, and increases confidence. Even modest work can significantly reduce future pressure.

Earning while learning is leverage.

Scholarships, grants, and institutional resources are also part of strategic borrowing. Every dollar of free or earned money replaces a dollar of debt. Students who pursue these options aggressively borrow less and gain more control.

Effort today buys freedom tomorrow.

Strategic borrowing also requires an exit plan. Before accepting debt, students should understand how repayment will work, when it begins, and what the monthly impact will be. Borrowing without an exit strategy is gambling with your future.

Clarity reduces fear.

The goal of strategic borrowing is not perfection. It is alignment. When debt aligns with purpose, values, and future capacity, it loses its power to harm. Students who master this approach graduate with confidence, not regret.

In the next chapter, we'll focus on how to build credit responsibly during college—using access wisely so that credit strengthens your future instead of undermining it.

Borrow intentionally.
Graduate empowered.

Chapter 8

Building Credit Without Destroying Your Future

Credit is not character.
But it can influence your options.

For many students, credit feels mysterious—
something important, powerful, and intimidating
all at once. It is often treated as a score to chase
rather than a system to understand. As a result,
students either avoid credit entirely or use it
recklessly, unaware that both extremes can limit
future opportunity.

Credit is not a reward.
It is a record.

Your credit profile tells a story about how you manage responsibility over time. It does not measure intelligence, ambition, or worth. It measures consistency. Understanding this shifts how credit should be approached during college—not as a shortcut to lifestyle, but as a long-term foundation.

Building credit responsibly does not require debt. It requires discipline.

One of the most damaging myths students believe is that carrying a balance improves credit. It does not. Credit scores are influenced by payment history, utilization, length of credit, and consistency—not interest paid. Interest benefits lenders, not borrowers.

You can build strong credit without ever paying interest.

Responsible credit use starts with restraint. A single, low-limit card is often enough. The purpose is not spending power—it is behavior tracking. Using credit for small, predictable expenses and paying it off in full builds trust without creating dependency.

Credit should be used deliberately, not emotionally.

Utilization is one of the most misunderstood factors in credit scoring. High balances—even if paid on time—signal risk. Keeping balances low relative to limits communicates control. This discipline matters more than income or access.

Control beats capacity.

Credit also influences more than loans. It can affect housing options, insurance rates, employment screenings, and even utilities. These consequences are rarely explained when credit is first offered, but they shape adult life quietly and persistently.

Your future self, lives with today's patterns.

Students who build credit well understand that access is not the goal—flexibility is. Strong credit creates options, not obligations. It allows you to choose when and how to borrow later, rather than being forced to accept unfavorable terms.

Options are power.

Just as important is learning when *not* to use credit. Credit should never be the solution to under-earning, overspending, or emotional stress.

Using credit to patch financial gaps trains dependence. Using it to track discipline trains strength.

Habits outlast balances.

Building credit during college is not about maximizing limits or chasing scores. It is about proving reliability over time. Students who approach credit with patience and purpose graduate with leverage instead of liability.

In the next chapter, we'll explore how to reduce borrowing by leveraging campus resources, income opportunities, and overlooked forms of financial support—strategies that replace debt with access.

Credit is a tool.
Wisdom determines how it's used.

Chapter 9

Leveraging Campus Resources Instead of Debt

Most students borrow more not because they must—but because they don't know what already exists.

College campuses are filled with resources designed to reduce financial pressure, yet many students overlook them. Not out of laziness, but out of unawareness. When debt feels easier than asking questions or seeking support, borrowing becomes the default solution.

But access is not the same as effort.

Universities quietly provide forms of financial leverage that cost nothing but attention and initiative. Scholarships, grants, emergency funds, academic stipends, work-study programs, tuition waivers, and departmental awards often go unused simply because students never apply. The assumption is that these opportunities are limited or unattainable. In reality, many are underutilized.

Free money favors the informed.

Work-study programs are often misunderstood. Many students dismiss them as low-paying or inconvenient, but these roles are strategically valuable. They offer income without sacrificing academic flexibility. They place students in environments that support learning rather than distract from it. Most importantly, they replace borrowed dollars with earned ones.

Earning while enrolled reduces pressure after graduation.

Internships offer another form of leverage. Paid internships not only reduce borrowing—they increase future earning potential. They build skills, networks, and confidence that translate into job offers and higher starting salaries. Even unpaid internships, when paired with stipends or academic credit, can outperform loans in long-term value.

Experience compounds faster than interest.

Campus resources also extend beyond money. Free tutoring, counseling, career services, and academic advising reduce costly mistakes. Dropping classes, changing majors repeatedly, or extending graduation timelines often leads to additional borrowing. Support systems exist to help students avoid these setbacks, but they only work when used.

Avoiding mistakes saves more than earning more.

Many students borrow because they underestimate their ability to generate income. Skills developed in the classroom—writing, design, technology, organization, communication—are monetizable long before graduation. Freelancing, tutoring, assisting faculty, or supporting campus departments can produce income while reinforcing education.

Debt is not the only option.

Leveraging campus resources requires initiative, not perfection. It requires asking questions, visiting offices, applying repeatedly, and accepting help without shame. This mindset shift alone can reduce borrowing dramatically.

Resourcefulness is a financial skill.

Students who replace debt with access graduate with confidence and clarity. They understand how systems work. They learn to seek opportunity instead of defaulting to obligation. This approach builds resilience that outlasts college.

In the next chapter, we'll focus on cash flow—why income during college often matters more than refunds, and how even modest savings create long-term financial advantage.

Knowledge unlocks resources.
Action turns them into freedom.

Chapter 10

The Power of Cash Flow While in School

Cash flow is not about how much money you have.
It's about how much control you have.

Many students believe financial stability begins after graduation, once a full-time salary arrives. In reality, the habits that determine stability are formed long before then. Cash flow during college—however small—creates momentum that debt never can.

Income changes behavior.
Debt delays it.

When students rely entirely on borrowed money, spending feels detached from effort. There is no immediate feedback loop. But when income is earned, even modestly, every dollar carries weight. Decisions become intentional. Awareness increases. Discipline develops.

Cash flow builds accountability.

Even a small, consistent income can transform a student's financial trajectory. It reduces reliance on credit. It replaces refunds with responsibility. It allows for saving—something many students believe is impossible during college.

Saving is not about amount.
It's about habit.

Students who save even a small percentage of income while in school develop a mindset of ownership. They learn that money can be directed instead of reacted to. Over time, this habit compounds into confidence and control.

Confidence reduces costly mistakes.

Cash flow also provides flexibility. Unexpected expenses—books, fees, transportation, emergencies—no longer require borrowing. When cash is available, debt becomes optional instead of automatic.

Options create peace.

Time management is often the barrier students fear most. But work that aligns with academic schedules—campus jobs, tutoring, freelance projects, internships—often reinforces discipline rather than undermining it. When work supports education, it enhances focus and purpose.

Purpose sharpens performance.

The most powerful advantage of cash flow during college is not financial—it is psychological. Students who earn while learning see themselves differently. They begin to understand their value. They realize they are not powerless or dependent. This identity shift influences every future decision.

Identity shapes outcomes.

Graduating with savings, however modest, creates momentum. It reduces fear. It increases confidence. It allows students to approach repayment, relocation, or career transitions from a position of strength instead of stress.

Debt demands urgency.
Cash flow creates strategy.

In the next chapter, we'll focus on preparing for life after graduation—understanding repayment, avoiding common mistakes, and transitioning into adulthood with clarity rather than panic.

Cash flow is not a distraction.
It is a foundation.

Chapter 11

Exit Strategy: Graduating Without Panic

Graduation is not freedom if you're financially unprepared.
It's exposure.

For many students, graduation day feels like victory—until the emails start arriving. Loan servicers begin contacting you. Grace periods quietly expire. Payments appear where excitement once lived. What was once invisible suddenly becomes unavoidable.

This is where panic is born.

Most graduates don't struggle because they borrowed. They struggle because they **never built**

an exit strategy. They knew how to enroll. They knew how to accept aid. But no one taught them how to leave college financially intact.

An exit without a plan is not an exit. It's a collision.

Student loan repayment does not begin when you feel ready. It begins on schedule—whether your income is stable or not. Many graduates assume they'll "figure it out" once they get a job, but jobs don't always come immediately, and salaries rarely stretch as far as expected.

Reality moves faster than optimism.

One of the most dangerous mistakes graduates make is ignoring their loans during the grace period. This window is not a break—it's a warning. Interest may still be accruing. Repayment options are being locked in. Decisions made during this time can add or subtract years of financial pressure.

Silence is expensive.

Income-driven repayment plans can be powerful tools—or long-term traps—depending on how they are used. Lower payments provide relief, but they can also extend debt for decades if not managed intentionally. Paying less feels good now, but it often costs more later.

Short-term comfort should never steal long-term freedom.

Deferment and forbearance are often misunderstood as solutions. In reality, they are pauses—not progress. Interest continues. Balances grow. Many borrowers look up years later shocked by numbers they never expected to see.

What you delay, you pay for—with interest.

Graduating without panic requires confronting the numbers early. Knowing your balances. Understanding your servicers. Estimating realistic payments. Matching lifestyle choices to income, not expectations.

Hope is not a plan.
Clarity is.

The graduates who thrive are not always the highest earners. They are the most prepared. They budget before their first paycheck arrives. They resist lifestyle inflation when income increases. They attack debt intentionally instead of emotionally.

Preparation beats salary every time.

An exit strategy also includes mindset. The transition from student to professional is jarring. Many graduates feel pressure to "finally enjoy life" after years of sacrifice. This is where financial collapse often begins—when freedom is confused with spending.

Freedom is control, not consumption.

Graduation should not feel like financial suffocation. It should feel like alignment. When students understand their obligations and options before they walk across the stage, they step into adulthood with confidence instead of fear.

**Debt does not define your future.
Avoidance does.**

In the next chapter, we'll confront a critical question every graduate must answer: Should you eliminate debt as fast as possible—or should you optimize it while building wealth?

Your next move determines the next decade.

Chapter 12

Debt Elimination vs. Debt Optimization

Not all debt should be treated the same.
And not all debt should be attacked the same way.

Many graduates are given one message: *"Pay it off as fast as possible."* Others hear the opposite: *"Don't worry about it—invest instead."* Both messages are incomplete. The real question is not whether to eliminate debt or optimize it. The question is **when, how, and why.**

Blind urgency creates mistakes.
Blind comfort creates stagnation.

Debt elimination is powerful. Paying off balances removes pressure, increases cash flow, and

75

restores peace. For many graduates, especially
those with high-interest or emotionally stressful
debt, elimination is the fastest path to stability. It
creates clarity and momentum.

**But elimination without strategy can slow
growth.**

Debt optimization, on the other hand, focuses on
balance. It recognizes that not all debt carries the
same risk. Low-interest, structured debt may be
managed while income increases, savings are built,
or investments are made. Optimization is not
avoidance—it is sequencing.

Sequencing determines speed.

The danger lies in misunderstanding optimization.
Many people use it as justification for delay. They
say they are "leveraging" debt while making no

progress in income, savings, or discipline. That is not optimization—that is denial.

Optimization requires discipline.
Without discipline, it becomes decay.

High-interest debt demands urgency. It bleeds resources and restricts flexibility. This kind of debt should be eliminated aggressively. Low-interest, predictable debt requires evaluation. Can your income comfortably support it? Is it preventing growth—or allowing it?

Debt must be assessed, not assumed.

Graduates must also consider emotional weight. Some debt creates constant stress, even if the math suggests patience. Peace matters. A strategy that looks good on paper but causes anxiety often leads to poor decisions later.

Financial progress is not just numerical—it is psychological.

The strongest financial strategies combine elimination and optimization. They remove toxic debt quickly while managing structured debt intentionally. They increase income before increasing lifestyle. They build savings while reducing balances. They move forward without extremes.

Extremes feel productive.
Balance creates sustainability.

This chapter is not about choosing sides. It is about choosing **wisdom**. Your strategy should evolve as your income, goals, and life stage change. What makes sense in your first year out of college may not make sense five years later.

Flexibility is strength.

Graduates who win financially are not reactive.
They do not chase trends or compare timelines.
They build a plan and adjust it as life unfolds.
They use debt as a variable—not a master.

In the final chapter, we'll focus on designing a future that outgrows debt entirely—building a financial identity that prioritizes freedom, purpose, and long-term legacy over short-term relief.

Debt is a chapter.
It does not have to be the story.

Chapter 13

Designing a Debt-Light, Power-Driven Future

Your future will not be defined by what you owed.
It will be defined by what you built.

Debt is not the final chapter—it is the proving ground. What matters most is not how much debt you carried through college, but what you decided to do *after* awareness arrived. This chapter is about reclaiming authorship over your financial life and refusing to drift into a future designed by defaults, pressure, or fear.

Drift is expensive.
Design is intentional.

Many graduates stumble financially not because they lack opportunity, but because they lack direction. Without a clear vision, income increases and debt payments coexist with lifestyle inflation, leaving people busy but not progressing. A debt-light future requires clarity before cash increases.

Clarity precedes freedom.

Designing your future begins with defining what *enough* looks like. Not socially. Not culturally. Personally. When you decide how much you actually need to live well, money stops controlling you and starts serving you.

Uncontrolled desire is more expensive than debt.

The first five years after graduation matter more than most people realize. These years' shape habits, expectations, and identity. Graduates who keep their lifestyle modest while income grows create a gap—between what they earn and what they spend. That gap is where power lives.

Margins create momentum.

A debt-light future is built by prioritizing flexibility over image. It means choosing freedom before luxury, progress before applause, and discipline before comfort. These decisions are rarely celebrated—but they compound quietly and powerfully.

Quiet discipline creates loud results.

Income should be directed, not reacted to. Raises, bonuses, and side income should fuel goals, not inflate lifestyle. This is how debt loses relevance over time—not through panic, but through strategy.

Strategy outlasts motivation.

A power-driven future also requires identity alignment. You are no longer a student surviving semester to semester. You are a builder. A steward. A decision-maker. When your identity shifts, your behavior follows.

Who you believe you are determines how you use money.

Debt does not disappear overnight, but its influence does when your income, savings, and discipline outgrow it. Eventually, debt becomes background noise instead of a daily concern. That is not luck—it is design.

Freedom is built, not granted.

This book was never about fear. It was about awareness. You were never behind—you were simply uninformed. Now you are equipped to make decisions that protect your future instead of borrowing against it.

Graduate with clarity.
Live with intention.
Build with power.

Your degree opens doors.
Your financial discipline determines
how far you walk through them.

Closing Reflection

Your Financial Life Begins Now!

You have reached the end of this book—but you are standing at the beginning of your financial life.

What you've gained here is not just information. It is **vision**. You now see what many people don't realize until years later: debt is not destiny, money is not mastery, and independence is not accidental. It is chosen.

From this moment forward, you are no longer allowed to say, *"I didn't know."*
That sentence no longer belongs to you.

You understand how debt works, how it sneaks in quietly, how it feeds on emotion, and how it grows when left unmanaged. More importantly, you understand how to stop it—how to control it, outgrow it, and eventually leave it behind.

Awareness is a responsibility.

You are not behind because you borrowed. You are behind only if you refuse to change what you now understand. The past cannot be edited, but the future is still unwritten—and you hold the pen.

Choose intention over impulse.
Choose strategy over stress.
Choose freedom over appearances.

Financial independence is not reserved for the wealthy, the privileged, or the lucky. It belongs to those who decide early that they will not finance comfort with tomorrow's peace. It belongs to those who refuse to live their adult life paying for their younger self's lack of clarity.

Debt-free living is not about restriction—it is about **power**. Power to choose work without desperation. Power to move without fear. Power to say no without panic. Power to build without borrowing your peace.

Your income will grow.
Your options will expand.
But only if your discipline grows first.

You are the generation that can break the cycle. The generation that refuses to inherit financial confusion and pass it forward. The generation that understands money early and therefore lives freely later.

Let your degree open doors—but let your discipline decide how far you go.

Do not wait for the "right time."
Do not wait for more money.
Do not wait for permission.

Start now!

- Track your money.
- Question every debt.
- Build cash flow.
- Protect your credit.
- Design your future on purpose.

And when pressure comes—and it will—
remember this truth:

You are not poor.
You are powerful.
And power, when disciplined, creates freedom.

Walk forward with clarity.
Live with intention.
Build a future that no longer owes yesterday
anything.

Your financial independence is not ahead of you—it begins with the next decision you make.

Other Books by Rev. Darryl Bass

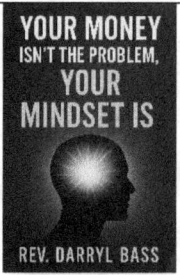	**Your Money Isn't the Problem, Your Mindset Is** A transformational work that challenges limiting financial beliefs and redefines wealth from the inside out, empowering readers to align their identity with abundance and responsibility.
	**This Is Why You're Broke** A bold and unapologetic examination of the habits, beliefs, and financial behaviors that keep people trapped in cycles of struggle. This book confronts uncomfortable truths and replaces excuses with execution,

	helping readers shift from reactive spending to strategic wealth building.
HEALING YOUR FINANCIAL TRAUMA PEOPLE CANNOT BUILD WHAT THEY STILL FEEL UNWORTHY OF	**Healing Your Financial Trauma** This book addresses the psychological and emotional roots of money struggles, helping readers break cycles, confront financial pain, and rebuild confidence and stability.
THE FINANCIAL IDENTITY SHIFT REBUILDING YOU BELIEVE YOU ARE WITH MONEY REV. DARRYL BASS	**The Financial Identity Shift** A mindset-and-behavior reset that helps readers align who they are with how they handle money, transforming financial habits through identity-based discipline.

	**The Life Progression System** A comprehensive blueprint for intentional living, The Life Progression System guides readers through structured personal growth, goal alignment, mindset transformation, and legacy building. It equips individuals with practical tools to move from drifting through life to deliberately designing it.
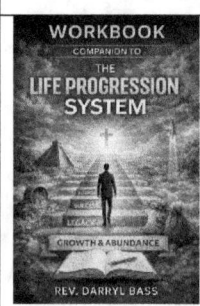	**The Life Progression System Workbook** A comprehensive blueprint for intentional living, The Life Progression System guides readers through structured personal growth, goal alignment, mindset transformation, and legacy building. It equips individuals with practical tools to move from drifting through life to deliberately designing it.

	**Financial Progression System** This book provides a step-by-step roadmap to financial stability and long-term wealth building. It teaches readers how to increase income, eliminate debt, build credit, create savings systems, and establish generational financial security.
	**Life Insurance: The Gift of Life After Life** More than a policy explanation, this book reframes life insurance as a strategic wealth-building and legacy-protection tool. It educates families on how to use life insurance for income replacement, debt protection, estate planning, generational wealth transfer, and financial leverage.

	**The Intellectual Property Wealth Blueprint** A strategic guide to turning knowledge into income, this book teaches creators how to package ideas into books, courses, systems, and assets that generate scalable and recurring revenue streams.
	**The Intellectual Property Wealth Blueprint 2.0** Focused on licensing, certification, and legacy systems, this volume expands intellectual property into scalable enterprises that create long-term wealth and generational ownership structures.

The Debt Eliminator

Coming 2026

What if 2026 was the year everything changed?

What if this was the year you stopped surviving...
and started building?
The year you stopped juggling bills... and started
creating wealth?
The year debt stopped controlling your decisions?

The **Debt Eliminator** is not another budgeting
class.
It is a structured financial transformation system
designed to help individuals and families break
free from consumer debt, rebuild financial
confidence, and establish a foundation for long-
term wealth.

This course was built for hardworking people who are tired of living paycheck to paycheck. It was created for families who want stability, not stress. It was designed for individuals who know they are capable of more—but need a system that works.

What the Debt Eliminator Will Teach You:

• How to eliminate consumer debt strategically and aggressively
• How to increase income without adding overwhelm
• How to rebuild and optimize your credit profile
• How to build savings while eliminating debt
• How to structure emergency funds and protection plans
• How to shift your financial identity from borrower to builder
• How to create systems that prevent debt from returning

This is not theory.
This is execution.

Through step-by-step modules, implementation tools, accountability structure, and real-life application, you will learn how to take control of your money instead of letting it control you.

Imagine waking up without financial anxiety.
Imagine having a plan.
Imagine watching your balances decrease and your confidence increase.
Imagine positioning your household for ownership, investing, and generational legacy.

That transformation begins in 2026.

The Debt Eliminator is more than a course.
It is a movement toward financial clarity, discipline, and freedom.

Get ready to break cycles.
Get ready to build stability.
Get ready to eliminate debt—permanently.

The Debt Eliminator —
Launching 2026.

Join our waiting list Today!
https://savingssolution.org/join

The Financial Freedom Revolution Tour

Launching 2026

This is not a seminar.
This is not a motivational rally.
This is a financial awakening.

The **Financial Freedom Revolution Tour** is a live, high-impact experience designed to ignite transformation in individuals, families, entrepreneurs, and communities ready to break financial cycles and build generational stability.

For too long, people have been working harder but falling further behind. Income rises. Expenses rise. Stress rises. Yet true financial progress feels out of reach.

The Revolution changes that.

This national tour brings together powerful teaching, real strategy, live coaching, and structured execution plans that move attendees from confusion to clarity—and from debt to disciplined wealth-building.

What You'll Experience:

• A clear roadmap to financial stability and long-term wealth
• Step-by-step strategies for eliminating consumer debt
• Income growth frameworks and entrepreneurship positioning
• Credit optimization and financial leverage strategies
• Protection planning and legacy-building principles
• Live financial assessments and actionable implementation steps
• A mindset shift from survival thinking to ownership thinking

This is not inspiration without structure.
This is strategy with accountability.

The Financial Freedom Revolution Tour is built for families who want peace instead of pressure. For entrepreneurs who want profit with structure. For leaders who understand that financial stability is the foundation for community impact.

Imagine thousands gathered in one space—learning, planning, committing to real change. Imagine leaving with a clear blueprint instead of just excitement. Imagine knowing exactly what steps to take the next day.

This is more than an event.
It is a declaration that debt cycles end here.
It is a call to financial responsibility, ownership, and generational leadership.

Cities across the country will host this movement in 2026.

Seats will fill.
Lives will shift.
Legacies will be built.

The Financial Freedom Revolution Tour — Coming 2026.

This is the year you stop reacting to money …and start commanding it.

The revolution begins with one decision.
https://savingssolution.org/tour

Follow on Social Media

Facebook:

https://www.facebook.com/LPSCoach

Twitter:

https://twitter.com/LPS_Coach

Instagram:

https://www.instagram.com/lps_coach/

YouTube:

https://www.youtube.com/@life_progression_system

TikTok:

https://www.tiktok.com/@debt_annihilator

LinkedIn:

https://www.linkedin.com/in/lpscoach/

www.ingramcontent.com/pod-product-compliance
Lightning Source LLC
Chambersburg PA
CBHW071323220526
45468CB00001B/480